FOUR MAGICAL SECRETS TO BUILDING A FABULOUS FORTUNE!

By T.J. Rohleder
(A.K.A. America's "Blue Jeans Millionaire")
Founder of the Direct-Response Network

Also by T.J. Rohleder:

Introduction

Greetings! I'm T.J. Rohleder, the founder of the Direct-Response Network and co-founder of M.O.R.E. Incorporated in Goessel, Kansas.

In this book I'm going discuss some fantastic tips and strategies that you can use to make enormous sums of money.

At M.O.R.E. Inc. these magical marketing tricks, as I call them, have helped us earn more than $113 million in 20 years -- so they're tested and proven methods of making money. Before I get started, though, I'd like to mention a couple of things that are really close to my heart.

Doing What It Takes

If you've ever read any of my literature, listened to one of my audio presentations, or heard me speak in person, you've probably encountered the following statement in one form or another: **"The only way you can really tell anything about a person is by the actions they take."** You may even be tired of getting that same message over and over again -- but I think it bears repeating. You see, a lot of people are great at talking. They talk a mean game, they claim they want to make millions of dollars -- but do they really? **We run into people all the time who really believe they want to make millions; and yet you ask them what they're doing to realize that dream, you discover that they're not doing a thing**. They don't even have any plan to get where they want to go.

That's the easy part, though. Having a good, solid plan is not the problem; all it takes is a little brain sweat to develop one. **What's important is what you find out when you ask them what they're doing to actually make that dream come true -- what they're willing to do, or what kind of actions they're taking.** That's where the chaff is separated from the wheat, the sheep from the goats. Some people are really great at making excuses. <u>But if you want to make millions of dollars, you can't make excuses</u>. People who make fortunes have one big thing in common: they don't make excuses. So you can't make excuses either. The more money you want to make, the more you have to be willing to do to get that money. **That's the secret to getting rich -- the willingness and the ability to do whatever it takes**.

Now, that sounds simple, and yet most people have never figured it out. If you want to make millions, you have to be willing to pay the price to earn it, to learn to do whatever it takes to turn small sums of money into a huge fortune. That's the theme of this Special Report.

The Golden Rule of Marketing

If you've got any experience at all in the marketing field, you've probably heard about the 80/20 Rule. **Basically, it states that you get 80% of your work from 20% of your workforce.** Some people have even called that the 95/5 Rule, which suggests that 5% of the people do 95% of the work. That's true of both business and entrepreneurship. Similarly, they say that something like 95% of new businesses go under within the first five years; there's an enormously high failure rate. **And yet, you tend to see patterns and trends develop when you look closely at the 5% who succeed.** My goal here is to reveal some of the secrets that generate those trends. If you're reading this Report, and you're serious about making large sums of money, then know that you have to strive to be part of that 5%. Just by reading this Report and taking it seriously, you're joining an elite club -- that small group of people who are absolutely committed to success. **You're not just a talker; you're a doer.**

If somehow you're reading this Report and you're not taking what I'm telling you seriously, then I have a challenge for you. Are you serious about marketing? Are you serious about making the most money? If you're not, go ahead and put this Report aside. Just put it away, stick it in a drawer somewhere, and forget it. **Hopefully someday, somehow, you'll figure out a way to be successful**.

Let's be blunt here. If you want to make the most money, you've got to be a doer: you've got to be somebody who goes out there and grabs success by the hand. That's what this Report is all about. What I'm going to discuss here has a lot do with magic, frankly -- hence the title. Now, when you consider stage magicians, you know that the key to their success is that they have to be believable. If they are, you sit there amazed at their performance -- but you know that their magic isn't real, that there's some sleight-of-hand and misdirection involved. **Yet magical marketing is true magic, in the sense that there really are formulas and secrets you can use to make a lot of money, to be truly successful in marketing and business.** If you're watching from the sidelines, it can seem like pure magic; it may seem like it's impossible. And yet, if you know the secret, you can be super-successful and make all the money, and enjoy all the success, that's been eluding you.

Believe it or not, I really am going to reveal my magical marketing tricks -- the secrets that take you behind the scenes and show you how it really is possible to turn small amounts of money into a fortune. It can all be done by becoming a great marketer. That's the basis of the secret that's made me and my company more than $113 million in just 20 years, and it's the secret that can make you the fortune you want. **No matter how much money you desire, it's all out there waiting for you right now**. It's in the pockets, purses, bank accounts, and credit card authorizations of millions of people who are just waiting to give you their money in exchange for something that you can offer, something they perceive as being worth far more than the money you're asking for in return.

Magical Marketing Secret #1

Give 'Em What They Want

Here's a magic marketing secret that, when done right, pulls in cash-paying customers faster and easier than you ever imagined possible. Now, the secret behind it is going to sound very simplistic, but I really have to explain it because, as they say, common sense isn't so common. **Basically, this magic marketing trick involves speaking directly to the wants of your customer or prospect, the person you're marketing to.** Sounds easy, doesn't it? But while most people understand it, they don't do it.

Let's use realtors as an example. If I'm looking for a realtor to help me sell my home or help me buy a new home, I've got specific wants, right? I've got a problem, so I'm going to go out and try to find someone to address that problem. **Now, if you look at most realtor advertising, do their headlines say something like, "Are you desperately looking to sell your house in the next 30 days? If so, here's the solution!"** Absolutely not! What do the headlines of 99.9% realtor ads say? Something like "Mary Jones," "Todd Wilson," or "Bob Franklin."

These realtors use their own names as the headline and slap their pictures up there next to it. How egotistical is that? I can't tell you how many billboards I've driven by for realtors where you don't even know they're a realtor, because, basically, it's a huge picture of somebody and their name and a slogan that says something like, "We're here for you." **Well, here for what?**

Sure, I might have a problem you can solve. I may even be willing to give you money to solve it. But unless you're going to connect with me and let me know how you're going to help me, there's no way I'm going to be doing business with you.

What I suggest is that whenever you're selling something, take yourself out of the equation. I know that's going to be difficult for a lot of people, because whenever we do marketing we believe we need to brand ourselves -- to put our face and name out there for people to remember. Well, let me turn that around. If you're able to solve somebody's problem, they'll get to know you. You'll be branded based on the result you were able to provide them. So don't go out there and throw your picture and your name onto your marketing materials, hoping to build your brand. **That's not how it works at all.**

The first thing you want to do is connect

with your customers and prospects, and really determine what it is <u>they</u> want. Not what it is that you want, or think they should want, but the real deal. And let's go deeper than just that: close your eyes and imagine that you're the prospect. Imagine that you have the exact same experiences; imagine what their daily life is like, the house that they live in, the income they make, whether they're married or unmarried, what their schedule is like, what their frustrations are like…<u>really put yourself in their shoes</u>. That's going to be very difficult for most marketers to do, because we're so used to saying, "Okay, we want to sell them this. We want to push something on them."

But what you really want to be in the business of is providing not products, but solutions. The best way you can communicate with your prospects is by figuring out what their exact problem is, and what their perception of it is. If you can put yourself into their life and their mindset, you can speak exactly to that problem, and offer an exact solution. **Putting yourself in their shoes enables you project outwards and realize that everybody in your particular market has this particular problem in common, and the person you're acting as is an avatar that allows you identify with that group.**

Then what you're going to do is say to

yourself, "Okay, if I were this person having this problem and I were going to take action, what would I do? Where would I go? Would I call a friend? Would I go to the Yellow Pages? Would I log onto the Internet? If I went onto the Internet, where would I go? Would I go to Google to do a search? If so, what would my search terms be?" Well, I'll tell you one thing -- if I were you, **I almost certainly wouldn't be looking for a particular product; <u>I'd be looking for a solution to my problem, whatever form it came in</u>**.

Once you've done this, you've effectively put yourself into the mind of the prospect. **You're looking for a solution to your problem, which is something most marketers don't think of.** Put yourself in their shoes at the exact time they have that problem, project yourself forward to see what actions they're taking and what they're looking for, and then create a sales message that speaks directly to their wants -- to their problems. **Take your name, your picture, and your product out of the equation, and give them the solution they need**.

Let's go back to the realtor example. If you're a realtor, what you want to say in your marketing message is something like, "Are you having a hard time finding a realtor you can trust to sell your house?" Or, "Would you like to sell your house in the next 30 days or less, guaranteed?" Or, "How would you like to start promoting your house today, within the next 30 minutes, and have it sold within the next 30 days, guaranteed -- or I'll buy your house from you?" **If someone selling a home had those challenges and saw that headline above and beyond your name, <u>they'd be interested, because you're providing that solution</u>.** This can happen in any and every market, with any type of prospect. Again, it sounds like common sense -- but nonetheless, most people get away from that. We marketers like the excitement of the product, and we like putting our names and our great sales messages out there. But the truth is, you can connect more with your prospects, make more sales, and create a better relationship by first putting yourself in the mind of the prospect and then delivering exactly what they want in terms of the marketing message.

Most people we work with come to us with specific products and services they want to sell, and that's all they want to talk about. They ask, "How can I get this product or service into the hands of the people I want to sell it to?" And then they have this crazy idea that everybody's going to be as much in love with what they're selling as they are. But that's the wrong attitude to take; we tell people to start with the market first. **That's the secret of our success.** Let's say somebody said to me, "Hey,

T. J., just give it to me on a 5 x 7 index card. What is it that really made you all the millions and millions of dollars you guys have brought in?" **I'd just tell them that it's all about empathy.**

For years before I struck it rich, I sent away for every single get-rich-quick program that I could find. I was on all of the mailing lists, and I got ripped off and lied to and cheated so many times. But when we finally did find a plan and a program that really, truly worked, and we offered that to the millions of people out there in the opportunity market, we knew their story and they knew ours. We were them and they were us. It's just that simple. You start with the market first.

It's hard to drill that into people's heads because they feel it's only natural that that marketing is all about the product first. But you have to get rid of that idea because the product is only a small part of it. **Marketing is about the consumer, first and foremost, and the biggest benefits they'll get from your product.** Even more than that, and even before that, it's about what they want -- what their needs and problems are. **You can start with knowing who you're dealing with, and the kinds of things they need fixed.** Then look at all the other people selling to that same clientele. What are they not providing that those people want? From there, you can find an appropriate product.

Maybe that product is something that you create yourself, especially if you're an information marketer. Maybe you buy the rights to a product that someone else has already created; there are all kinds of Joint Venture opportunities out there. When you get right down to it, there are all kinds of ways you can actually get a product into people's hands -- but you always start with the group of people that you want to sell to, and then figure out what their challenges are and what kinds of products they want the most. **If there's tons of pressure in the marketplace, then that means there's a huge opportunity for you to fill that need, meet that demand, rise to that challenge, and make a lot of money doing it.** To repeat: it all starts not with the product, but the prospect.

I realize that a lot of people who read this -- especially those with business degrees -- are going to look at it and say, "Hey now, that's way too simple, T.J." **But the truth is, the simplest things are usually the most effective**. Too often, we try to make marketing and business a lot more complicated than it has to be. Business isn't about all these complex theories and concepts you learn in business school; if it was, wouldn't those professors teaching them be wealthy entrepreneurs instead of making do with maybe $50,000 a year? **No, business is all about delivering solutions to people who have problems**. That's a powerful reality because, if you've got a target market consisting of people who've all got a similar problem and you have a solution for them that really works -- well, it's going to make a connection and you're going to make so much money by offering them that solution that you'll be blown away.

Here's a particularly ravenous example: the weight-loss market. Now, these people don't care about the name of your product. They don't care about who you are, or the history of your company, or how long you've been in business. **They care about results**. They want to lose weight. They want to do it as fast and as easily as possible. So if you have a product that delivers that solution, then you're going to make a good connection with that market because that's precisely the solution your market wants.

Too many people start with the product; they say, "Okay, I've got a great idea, and I'm sure it's going to sell to everybody," and they go out and spend weeks or months or, heaven forbid, years creating this product. Then they take it to the market they think is going to buy it and BOOM…nobody buys it and they're scratching their heads wondering, "Okay, why didn't this work?" **Well, it didn't work because they did things the hard way and put the cart before the horse.** Once again, the simple way to succeed is to go to the market first, find out what they want, find out what their problems are, find out what they're willing to pay to solve those problems, and then create exactly that product -- based only on what they want.

But if it's so simple, why aren't more people doing that? **Like I said: it's because common sense is uncommon.** Entrepreneurs tend to be very smart people, even though we sometimes do stupid things. **Our biggest problem is that we tend to complicate everything.** Instead of doing that, just find the biggest frustrations in the marketplace, and determine how you can solve them instantly. You'll make money like magic.

At M.O.R.E., Inc., we're currently developing some products and services that are designed for business owners. We know what kinds of things we want to sell to these business owners, sure -- but it's not about what we want to sell to them. **It's about what they're looking for, and it's about understanding their biggest problems**. You see, in a very general sort of way, people want relief from some kind of pain that they're in. Let's consider the weight-loss industry again. People who want to lose weight are in great emotional trauma. It's all they think about, constantly! People who want to make a lot of money are in a similar situation. It's all they think about, and they're often frustrated, so there's a

---

certain amount of tension here. The kind of people that we're trying to reach -- the 12-30 million business owners in America -- have all kinds of problems and frustrations and pressures. These are the things that keep them awake at night, the things that get them out of bed in the morning, the things that just drive them crazy. **So what we have to do is develop products and services that are centered around their biggest problems.** Our ability to get their money is based on our ability to meet their needs, to solve their problems.

It's as simple as that, but I don't want to you to think it's necessarily easy. **We're tearing our hair out trying to make this thing work, and that's how it goes with a lot of markets.** There's nothing easy about it -- but once you know how rock-bottom simple the basic concept is, that helps keep you focused. That's really the key. You start with the simple concept, and then you realize, "Okay, I've got to dig down and figure out what my market wants." Saying that is easy -- but actually accomplishing it is a whole other deal. **It takes a lot of hard work.** With the business products we're looking at, you're talking about interviewing or surveying hundreds of people, in order to see exactly what it is they're looking for. That's another thing -- you've got to stay in touch with your market at all times. **If you don't maintain that link, no matter how high you get in the business, you'll lose touch with what's important.** You may think you've still got an idea of what all these people want when, in reality, you may have no clue.

I've had that problem in my own business. I've found myself thinking, "Okay, I know where I've come from, and I still kind of remember it." **But let's be honest: if it's 5, 10, or 20 years since you've been in a particular position, some of that intensity has died down.** So what I'll do nowadays is try to go to seminars and speak to my own customers and clients. I'll go to similar seminars that are being sold to people in my market, and just look at the people there, and talk to the ones interested in products that are similar to mine. I've been doing surveys to people on my mailing list, where I actually ask them, "What are you interested in? What's your biggest challenge? What's your biggest problem?" **I even tell them, "I'm looking for a problem outside of what my market can offer you, or what even my company can offer you."** We develop products and opportunities that help people quit their jobs and work for themselves, but I ask people, "Okay, I want you to tell me all your problems. It doesn't matter if it's back pain, if it's relationship problems, what are those problems? Because I want to have such a great understanding of where you're at that I'm able to develop solutions to those problems." And it's interesting, in doing those surveys, to discover that I'm getting quite a lot of deep information…deeper than I, personally, would have expected. But it's helping me develop products and services and opportunities that really match the market.

So, again, it's a simple concept: give your market what it wants. It may very well take some legwork to actually connect with the market, to really find out what they want. But believe me: make that connect with your market, and it'll pay off over time.

Crushing the Competition

So let's say you've studied your marketplace, you've developed a product that solves their problem and meets their needs, and you're starting to make money. You're competing on a daily basis. **But if you want to make the real money, you're going to have to be ruthless -- you need to be willing to crush your competition.** Here's one way to do that, and end up quadrupling your profits.

Again, it sounds absurdly simple, and it is: you give away a free item. But this one free item is so powerful that it gives you the opportunity to literally blow your competition out of the water and dominate your market. It's an item that can be relatively inexpensive to create and give away -- and you definitely want to give it away. By now you're probably thinking, "Okay, what is this one free thing? Is it a CD? Is it a Report? What is it?"

It's education. It's information.

A lot of marketers (myself included) have been guilty of just giving you all the sizzle with our

---

marketing, and none of the steak. Well, the sizzle's important, so we get you hyped up. We tell you how great a product is. We give you all the bullet points; we give you a great headline; we tease and tease until you're salivating because you want the product so bad. And then, at the end, we let you buy the product and you rush to get it. Right? That's how a lot of marketers work. And, personally, that's how I've done it over the years, at times.

But you can crush your competition and make much, much more money if, along with the free sizzle, you'll also deliver part of the steak. **If you're willing to give up some of your best information before your prospect pays you a cent, then you have the ability to create a strong bond with your market -- <u>because everybody else is only giving them the sizzle</u>.** They're not providing any meat and potatoes information. But let's say you're doing just that. You're willing to give them an actual trick, a technique, something that will really work for them before they buy from you. What will that do to the prospect? That gets them to want to buy the product from you. Why? Well, let me explain.

When somebody sees a sales letter, whether it's online, through Direct Mail, or as a full-page ad in a magazine, all they know is what you're saying about the product. **They don't have the ability to sample it, or to match what you say you're going**

---

to deliver with your marketing message. So in their own head, they've got to make a decision: "Okay, is this person hyping it up too much? Are they really going to deliver?" They don't know -- and they're probably cautious, because they've been disappointed before. So in some cases they're sitting on the fence wondering, "Should I or shouldn't I?" **And if there's one thing I know after 20 years, it's that a confused mind doesn't buy. But if you're willing to give up some of your valuable information, you're going to make the buying process a lot easier for that prospect.** Give them some of that information, and they're able to gauge the quality of what you have to offer them. If you've got great information, they're going to be able to see that, and they're probably going to go ahead and purchase. You're actually going to push the buying ahead just by being generous, <u>based on the fact that you're giving them some value</u>.

Now, I'm going to make this sound a little bit weird, but stick with me here. **A lot of marketers don't want to give up the good stuff.** They may be willing to give you a little taste of something, of course; they understand this concept of baiting the hook with a little bit of information, hoping to snag you and pull you in. But they don't want to give you the best stuff; they want to save that for the big product, the big seminar, or the big home study

---

course. But the truth is, holding back like that hurts them in the long run. What I would recommend that you do is give away the best stuff. **That's right: give away the best stuff.**

You take that one technique, that one method that really gives results quickly and easily, and you give that away free before the prospect actually buys. Now, you may say, **"T.J., that sounds insane! Why would we do that?"** <u>The reason is because of the psychology of the prospect</u>. You see, they'll believe that if you're giving away this solid gold information for free, well heck -- if they give you money, the information they're going to pay for has to be worth many, many times that amount. The logical assumption is that if you give them "C" quality information, what they can buy from you must be "C" quality information as well. But if you give them "A+" information free of charge, they're going to think, "Hey, if I got this one idea that's A+ information, then that whole course must be full of A+ information!" and you're going to push the sale ahead.

As you can see, this isn't about keeping stuff back. A lot of marketers will hold everything back and say, "No, no, no. Before you can get any of my stuff, you've got to hand over some money." What I'm saying to do is counter-intuitive. **What I'm saying to do is give them a little bit of your best**

information. Not all of it, of course, but a big bite. Share that with them. Show them you trust them, and that will prove to them that everything else you've got is high-quality information, too. It's a great concept that gives you the ability to create a bond with your prospect -- and I'd say 98% of marketers simply aren't willing to do it.

But put it to work in your business, and you'll end up crushing your stingy competition. That's because your prospects are realizing, "Wow, this person is willing to give me the best information right off the bat, for nothing! Obviously, all their other information is great, so I'm going to spend my money with them instead of all these other people who refuse to give me any information. They just want to sell me the sizzle…all the hype and the hoopla." And they're right. **If you can give away free audio information, free Reports, free videos, free CDs or DVDs with those good bites of information on them, <u>you really do have the ability to increase your sales and crush your competition</u>.**

Two of the things we're doing with the Direct Response Network illustrate this point very well. As you probably know if you're reading this, we've developed something called the Automatic Recruiting System for the DRN that gives away a program called "20/20 Wealth Vision." That program sells in our catalog for $495 -- and yet we're giving it away absolutely FREE with no strings attached, no gimmicks, no tricks, no fine print, no cost...nothing! It's available on the website for free. If you want to pay a $5.00 fee to help cover some of our costs, you can get the MP3 version. And then, if you want to spend just a little bit more money and get all nine audio CDs, it's pretty much at our cost. We don't make any profit on that.

Our newest program, which we haven't even officially launched yet, offers to give away our "Part-Time Riches" program -- that's $4,529 worth of products, all condensed to MP3. **There's no catch, though there is a condition that's attached to the offer: the program is free as a bonus with a specific sale**. So while there is that condition, there are no catches or tricks; we even let people keep the free programs if they return the main product. In doing this, we're just trying to blow people away! We're trying to separate ourselves from all the other people in the information market.

Earlier, I mentioned that about 98% of the people in any market are afraid to do this. To be honest, I think that's awfully generous -- the true figure is probably 99% or more. **Fear is a very big problem for most marketers.** They're afraid to give away their best stuff because they think that if they do, no one will spend any money with them. **They**

can't get their minds wrapped around the concept that people will want to buy more from you if what they get from you for free is of the highest quality. I can see where they're coming from, somewhat because in the real world, you don't go into a restaurant and get told the cheeseburger and fries is going to cost you $29.50, while the prime filet mignon is only $1.95. That doesn't happen -- it's alien to their experience. **The highest-priced stuff is always the best stuff.** That's why they just can't understand how you could give away the best stuff in order to get more people to do business with you. If you feel that way, you've got to make a major mental shift in how you think about business -- a paradigm shift, if you will.

Recently, I was involved in a discussion about movie trailers. In a lot of cases, if you watch a movie trailer on TV and then go see the movie, by the time it's over you're thinking, "Jeez, I feel like I already saw everything, because all the best parts were in the trailer." **They give away all the best parts, and that gets you to go see the movie.** It works outrageously well, doesn't it? If that two-minute trailer clip was of a boring scene from the middle of the movie, where it was kind of dragging, you'd be thinking, "Boy, I've got other things I could be doing instead of sitting here watching this horrible scene." **That's why they give away the best part, the high-action scenes, the things that make you sit**

---

on the edge of your seat. <u>That's what gets you to go to the movie</u>.

It's the same thing when you're selling your product. Give them the best stuff free, and that will make them salivate for the rest of what you have. That's not to say that the rest of what you have is trash; it's just that the best stuff is in the "trailer." **Pick the things that are going to make your customer salivate the most**. Deliver that information free and that will get them to come running to you with their wallets open, ready to give you whatever you ask to get the rest of the benefits you're guaranteeing through your offer.

Here are two strategies you can actually put into action. **The first one is this: if you're selling a print product, or even an eBook, give your prospects a free chapter or excerpt.** My colleague Jeff Gardner, who's one of the best marketers I know, has a book that he's selling online very successfully right now: it's called The 12 Month Millionaire. It wasn't written by Jeff; the author is a marketing expert by the name of Vincent James. **On his website, Jeff gives away the first chapter absolutely free.** One of the things Jeff requests is that the prospect requesting the free chapter include their name and email address; then he goes ahead and emails them the first chapter, word for word. Now, why would Jeff do that? **Simply because he**

knows that after they get done reading that very first chapter, which contains a lot of information, they're going to want to read the second, the third, the fourth, and on and on...every chapter of that book. Jeff isn't afraid to give away one chapter because he knows that giving them that valuable information -- an actual part of that product -- will make them want to purchase the rest of that product. So if you've got an information product, try giving away the best chapter, or even just the first chapter; in any case, give away some of that product, and then make sure they've got some way to go back and purchase the rest of it.

A second strategy relates specifically to email. A lot of people are overwhelmed with spam emails. They've got so many coming in that most marketing messages are going right into a kill file or trash can. **Well, here's a secret that makes people not only open your email, but actually look forward to it: make sure you give them valuable information in every message.** When Jeff Gardner sends out an email to his list, he always gives them a moneymaking strategy they can use: a technique or trick that will actually benefit them, something that will definitely get results and solve a problem if applied correctly. Sure, it's free of charge, but it's valuable information. **The reason Jeff does this is because his customers know that he does it in every single email...though, of**

course, at the end of those emails, he also includes marketing information about his product. But they don't mind the pitch because they always get something valuable with it -- and so whenever they see a Jeff Gardner email, they open it up first thing.

That's not the case for all those marketers who are just pitching a product and saying, "Hey, come to my website. We're doing this big launch." **Their emails get pitched into kill files and reported as spam -- whereas Jeff's get separated out because he's delivering real value.** Because he gives away that information, Jeff is able to get through all the clutter of marketing messages that people have learned to ignore. He's basically trained his list to think, "Hey, when Jeff emails you something you're going to get some value -- open it up!" **This dramatically increases the response rates for the product he's offering elsewhere in that email.** Giving away something can make your email list much more responsive.

It's all about separating yourself from the competition. My colleague, Russ von Hoelscher, tells a great story about the owner of a sandwich shop who came to him years ago and said, "Russ, our business is just going down the drain. Although we make the best sandwiches in San Diego, the neighborhood our little sandwich shop is in has sort

---

of…well, let's say it's turned seedy." All of a sudden prostitutes were hanging out in that neighborhood and people started opening "massage parlors" and the kind of movie theaters that don't show family films. The whole neighborhood had gone to hell, but this guy couldn't leave -- either he owned his real estate, or was locked into a long-term lease he couldn't get out of. **But there was a ray of hope: within a couple blocks of his sandwich shop were scores of high-rise office buildings.** So after Russ sampled his sandwiches, he told the owner, "Here's what you have to do…"

It was a simple idea, it was based on exactly what we're talking about here, and it completely turned that business around. All the owner did was hire some nice, attractive young women who were very well-dressed, very clean and neat and professional. Every single weekday, right before noon, they'd go to the nearby office buildings and deliver free samples of the sandwiches, along with a little menu card, and answer any questions people might have. I think they even eventually developed a delivery system, but that came later. **All they did in the beginning was give away hundreds of dollars worth of free food every week.** In response, they got thousands and thousands of dollars worth of repeat business from people who sampled the product, loved the sandwiches, and were willing to go through the type of neighborhood that they wouldn't necessarily want to enter if there wasn't something worthwhile at the other end.

I've always thought that was one of the greatest stories I've ever heard -- yet so many business owners don't catch the message because they think to themselves, "Well, I don't run a sandwich shop. I can't pass out sandwiches." But that's the great thing about the information business. **We have the ability to get information out to people very inexpensively, to give them that little sample of something great**. Actually, it's the same way with any business you're in. If I were a realtor, I could give away a Report on the ten things to definitely not do when selling your home -- or ten things to understand before you buy a new home. It's true if you're a carpet cleaner -- which is the business I started out in -- or a plumber or a lawyer. You can give away a little information to your prospects before they actually purchase from you. **By doing that, you're able to make that connection, set yourself apart, and pull prospects in, versus everybody else who's just showing them the marketing and advertising.** Here's the key point you should take away with you: <u>giving away information can work for every type of business</u>.

Earlier I mentioned that real estate agents

tend to create identical-looking ads, with their name and face right at the top. **Obviously, there's some benefit to having name recognition and you want to be known in your industry; but what benefit is your name or image offering?** People just scanning the listings, looking for a realtor, want to have a benefit. A lot of people running ads in the Yellow Pages could do themselves a huge service just by having someone who knows marketing re-write their ad and focus on offering a benefit: a free Report, some kind of giveaway, something they could do just to draw attention to their ad and make it look different than all the other ones running right next to it. But people don't even think that way. Unfortunately, they get bound into their particular market. **They forget they have all these competitors and that they have to do something strong to differentiate themselves from the crowd.** Everybody's running with the herd, doing the exact same thing, and wondering why they're not getting good results. Well, sometimes you have to do the thing that's counterintuitive. Do something different from everybody else and you'll really stand out above and beyond your competition.

Forget About Competing on Price

Here's a secret most marketers won't admit: competing on price doesn't really work, if only because that's usually one of the cases where everybody's following the follower. **Competing on price can kill your business**. It makes absolutely no sense because there's somebody in almost any market who's either crazy enough -- or who doesn't understand business enough -- to compete with everybody on price so vigorously that they even drive themselves out of business. You may find somebody out there who says, "I can beat your price, I can beat your price, I can beat your price," until they're out of business. Well, guess what? By then, you're probably out of business as well!

Don't compete on price! It's a losing proposition. The real secret to easily dominating your market is competing on everything else. You want to compete on service; you want to compete on quality; you want to compete on speed; you want to compete on ease; you want to compete on customer experience. **Whatever business you're in, you need to create a brainstorming sheet on every aspect of your business and find ways where you can deliver a 'wow' experience to the people in your market.** That is, you have to figure out how you can go above and beyond in everything you do, in terms of delivering your services or products so your customer says, "Wow! This company is phenomenal. I'm glad I'm doing business with them."

Because, yes, in any market you're going to have price shoppers. You're going to have people who buy only on price, and there's no way around that. **But at the same time, you also have people who buy based on experience, or who buy based on quality and speed.** So what I would recommend you do is not try to sell to your entire market. Put aside the people who are buying based on price and say, "Okay, I'm going to give up all those people to the marketers who are happy to compete on price, and let them drive each other out of business. From this day forward, I'm not competing on price. That part of the market is gone and invisible to me. I'll compete on everything else that I can deliver to my customers and prospects -- that 'wow' experience."

The reason you want to do that is because you're going to build up a clientele that's more loyal than you would if you were competing only on price. **Price shoppers aren't loyal; since the only thing they're interested in is price, they're going to jump around from company to company trying to find the best price**. If you get away from those people and deliver the best service, in the best time, and in the best quality, then you can build up a bond where your customers will come back and do business with you again and again for years to come.

But above and beyond that, if you give somebody a 'wow' experience -- if you deliver something that's absolutely phenomenal -- are people going to keep it to themselves? <u>No! They want to tell other people.</u> They love to tell stories to other people and say, "Hey, guess what? I just had this crazy experience with this company. I bought X, Y, Z product and they hand-delivered it on a silver platter." Or, "They sent it overnight, wrapped up in a red bow." Or, "They sent along a box of chocolates with it," or whatever that 'wow' experience is for your particular market. **People are going to share that, and it's going to generate more business, free of charge**.

You know, a lot of people in any business obsess about referrals. We tell ourselves, "Okay, we want our customers to go out and get us more customers." **If you're just doing an okay job and**

---

people are kind of satisfied, well, they're not going to go out of their way to bring you in more business. They're not going to talk about your company. Believe me, I do business with a lot of people, and almost all of them do a good job. But usually it's just a good job; there's no reason for me to say, "Hey, this company is phenomenal and you should do business with them." They're good. I figure they're as good as anybody else, so why talk them up? But believe me, when I have a 'wow' experience, when I have a phenomenal experience with a company, I'm telling everybody about it!

So whatever business you're in, whether you're selling information products, whether you're in carpet cleaning or real estate, just brainstorm out some 'wow' experiences. **Ask yourself, "How can I really impress people?"** And keep in mind that these are things that can be very, very simple.

Let me give you a brief example, using my friend Jeff Gardner again. He was recently telling me about a time, not too long ago, when he hired a plumber to come to his home and fix a clogged sink. This was a new plumber, because he'd been through maybe four or five others. These people were shoddily dressed and dirty and they had poor social skills, and Jeff was never really happy with them -- so he was always going to the next company, and then the next company when that

---

one didn't pan out. **Well, when Jeff called this new company, they sent somebody over who was very clean, pristinely dressed in a nice polo shirt embroidered with the company's logo, nice dress pants, and dress shoes.** This guy was top of the line. Before he came in, he introduced himself and showed Jeff his identification. Then he said, "Oh, if you could just wait right there a second, sir..." and he put on these pink booties. I know that sounds a bit strange, but they're just little cover-ups that go over the soles of your shoes with elastic. He put those on his shoes and he said, "I don't want to get anything on your carpet."

Now, that stuck in Jeff's mind and probably always will, because nobody before then had ever cared. They'd always drug in dirt and weeds and twigs and whatever and ground them into the carpet, and they never cared. **Right off the bat, Jeff got a great vibe from this gentleman.** He came in, did exactly what he said he was going to do at a great price, and he gave Jeff business cards and a magnet for the refrigerator. Jeff just had a phenomenal experience!

And so guess who he called the next time he had plumbing problems? A different company? No. **Jeff called that same company back, again and again, just because of a few simple things they do better than every other plumbing company in**

---

the area. Now he always does business with them, and he always recommends them to other people who are looking for a plumber.

I think that's a great story because it's so illustrative of what I'm trying to get across here with Magical Marketing Secret #3. **Think of ways you can give people a 'wow' experience, and at the same time keep away from competing on price -- because that can destroy your business.** People who are only looking for the lowest price aren't loyal customers you can keep for years anyway. A good impression can be far more effective than dropping your price into the basement. It doesn't even have to be that you spend more money than your competitors; you just have to do the small things right. <u>Give your customer a positive impression, offer them a good experience, and you'll be rewarded</u>.

If you have to compete on price, it usually means you're cutting costs somewhere. Obviously, every business exists to make a profit; but if you're making a small enough profit that you're competing on price, eventually you'll get to the point where there's no profit left. **So while I think price is a good thing to consider, you shouldn't attempt to make yours lower than everybody else's.** That's a recipe for disaster. When I first became self-employed, the only thing I knew how to do was have the lowest price; that was my degree of skill at the time, and in fact it was the only way that I knew how to get business. I was the cheapest date, so to speak, and that's all I would ever talk about in my marketing. But remember: price is only one thing out of many others to consider. It's a terrible thing to obsess with your price because, even if you're committed to giving good service -- which I was -- it's just not enough. I was the lowest priced competitor out there, so there wasn't enough money at the end of the day to give my customers the kind of service that they not only appreciated, but would then brag to all their friends about.

The Real Magic

And now, for my last trick! **It's called the "no-work, no-hassle way to making extra profits instantly."** I know that sounds like a lot of hype, but here's the way to do it: <u>include an upsell every single time you do any type of marketing</u>. When a customer is in the process of buying, ask them if they'd be interested in buying an additional item, or even multiple additional items. The best example I have of this is if you've ever bought anything off of an infomercial. You call up to buy the rotisserie or the pasta maker or the Ginsu knives and they take all your credit card and marketing information. Then, before you hang up, they try to add something else on. It could be almost anything: "Well, here's our Discount Buyers Club," or "Here's extra-fast shipping," or "Here's a monthly membership to a magazine or membership site," or any number of different things. **You need to apply that same upselling technique to everything you market.**

The reason I call this a no-work, no-hassle way to make extra profits instantly is because when this technique comes into play, you already have a

---

customer committed to buying something from you. So all you're doing is just adding one extra step. **It's not any extra hassle; it's really not any extra work.** You just add that extra step where you say, "Okay, you've bought A; how would you like B? Okay, you've bought A and B; how would you like C?" Just ask them at the point of purchase if they'd like to buy something else. You're going to have a certain percentage of people who add on whatever that other thing is, <u>so you automatically get additional money with no additional marketing costs</u>. Think about it: the marketing costs were already there. You've already paid to get that prospect to a website, or to send them your Direct Mail letter, or to have them come to your Yellow Pages ad. You've already paid for the marketing and they've already purchased. So when you offer them something else, it's at no additional cost to you.

Here's one of the ways that we use this method on the Internet. After the prospect clicks the "Buy" button to go ahead and commit to buying something, we take them to an upsell page where they can upgrade their purchase. We tell them something like, "By the way, before you continue further, we want to let you know about our Deluxe Package, which is only 10 or 20 percent more. We can ship it to you today for only X dollars." You can do that on an offline order form, too: "Oh, we've also got this brand new CD," or "Hey, we've got this brand new DVD set. How would you like to add it to your order?" **It's all about finding something that goes with whatever you're selling and adding it at the right point.** When you do that, you're adding money to your bottom line without any additional marketing costs. It's a quick, simple technique, a no-hassle way to increase your profits instantly without spending any additional money.

As I told you earlier, at M.O.R.E. Inc., we're currently developing products that go out to business owners, and the product we want to sell the most of costs around $5,000. Well, a lot of people who are brand new to us don't trust us enough yet to give us $5,000, and we know that. **We know that trust has to be earned.** There's a certain number of things you have to do to build a relationship with a client before you can ask them to give you $5,000. That's why we're using a stair-step kind of marketing strategy whereby we first try to sell our group of prospects more inexpensive products. **However -- and this is very important -- there are always people within that group of prospects who are like me: I do things so impulsively.** I'm the kind of person who's sometimes willing to just spend five grand and take a risk; in fact, I've spent a lot more than five grand, since I didn't need all the hand-holding or trust-building exercises that most people require of a company. So on all our order forms, even if we're

---

really focusing on selling them more inexpensive items, we put that $5,000 offer right there as an upsell, telling them to call a special number if they want it. That's because we know that a certain number of people will take that $5,000 offer right away. <u>That translates into instant profitability</u>.

It's been proven time and again that, with most upsells, you don't even need to explain the extra benefits in detail most of the time. Maybe you've got an upsell that's a couple hundred bucks, even, that just says, "Hey, we've got this package. Here's what it is…" You give them a paragraph about it on the order form, along with the title, and tell them what the regular price is. Then you say, "However, if you check this box on the form, we'll add it to your order for only this much." **If even a small percentage of your customers choose to take that upgrade, your upsell can put you in the black much faster than you expected.**

Conclusions

I want to thank you for taking the time to read this Special Report, and I hope you'll read it again and take notes. Every time you read it, I guarantee you you're going to see and understand things that you didn't catch previously. Also, I truly want to thank you for doing what so many people refuse to do -- and that's paying the price. I'm not a professional speaker or a writer; I'm not a professional entertainer in any form. I realize that it can be burdensome to get through some of these materials. I know this because I listen to my own tapes and read my own literature, and sometimes even I find it a hard slog. **But we don't try to kid ourselves here: we're trying to share the best secrets we can: real, effective secrets that can help you turn small amounts of money into a huge fortune**. While we like to say these secrets are magic, they really aren't the kind of magic that happens if you just snap your fingers and say "hocus pocus."

They won't work if you don't put in all the hard work to make them real. If you're paying the price by reading this Report again and again, listening to our audio presentations, or attending seminars, then what you're doing is building your knowledge, even if you don't realize it. And that's critical in the business because knowledge really is power.

The more you know, the more money you can make.